CUT AND SEW FA⌄⊓⊓⊍N

Brenda Redmile

SPAWTON BOOKS
32 Cherry Tree Avenue
Leicester Forest East
Leicestershire
LE3 3HN

Acknowledgements

My thanks to Elna Sewing Machines (GB) Ltd. and A.E Arthur Ltd. (Ardis Dressform) for their help and encouragement in the production of this book.

SPAWTON BOOKS
32 Cherry Tree Avenue, Leicester Forest East, Leicestershire LE3 3HN.
Published 1994
©Brenda Redmile

Cover design by Wendy Redmile

Printed by
Chatham Printers Ltd, Leicester

ISBN 0 9512458 3 X

CONTENTS

Introduction

BLOUSE/SHIRT BLOCK   7
Blouse block, sleeve block, tracing
the block, seams, hems and facings.

MAKING UP THE BLOUSE   17
Cutting and marking cloth, darts,
setting in sleeves, facing round neck,
buttonholes, hemming.

NECKLINES   24
Square neckline, sweet-heart neckline,
"V" neckline, scallop neckline.

COLLARS   30
Flat collar, one piece collar, shirt
collar, flounced collar, revers.

SLEEVES   42
Long full sleeve, puff and tulip sleeve,
flared short sleeve, contrast panel
sleeve, short sleeve with turn up cuff,
pleated sleeve.

PRINCESS LINE and WING SEAM   52
Princess line blouse, Princess line
dress, wing seam blouse.

POCKETS   58
Welt pocket, piped pocket, side panel
pocket, welt panel pocket.

YOKES   64
Shoulder yoke, false yoke, neck and
front yoke, back yoke.

SIZING UP FOR JACKET   70
Jacket block, wing seam jacket.

WAIST COAT   75
Gentleman's waist coat.

INTRODUCTION

Dress designers generally make patterns by using one of two different methods or a combination of both. The methods are known as "modelling" or "flat pattern making" and it is the flat method that is used in this book. This means that the styles are created from a basic flat pattern block using seams, darts and ease to mould the flat shape around the body. The basic pattern used throughout the book is for a blouse or shirt, but this may be adapted to a jacket or a full length dress. Once the block pattern is made to your own measurements all the various styles of necklines, collars, sleeves, yokes etc. may be made from the block enabling you to design the garments you wish to make rather than depending on the choice in the shops. As the basic block is cut to your own measurements you can be sure of a correct fit with each style you create. This avoids the necessity to keep dressing and un-dressing to fit the garment at every stage of making up. Instead you can cut and sew with the minimum amount of handling. A dress form (tailor's dummy) is useful to try your garments on especially as the more recent models are easily adjusted to a wide range of sizes. Try new styles in test cloth first and you will soon gain experience and be able to cut the shapes that are in fashion and, perhaps more importantly, are comfortable for you.

Dressmaking has never been easier with all the sewing aids on the market today to help you achieve a professional finish. However, do beware of unnecessary gimmicks which may not really help you and will certainly add to the cost of the garment you are making. Take note of how garments are made when they are hanging on rails in stores, then go home and make your own mix and match collection.

Equipment.

The basic equipment you will need for the pattern making is - scissors for cutting paper, pencils, eraser, tape measure, metre stick, set square, metal tracing wheel and plain pattern paper, (a roll of wall lining paper from DIY shops is the cheapest pattern paper available), thin card for making the blocks and sticky tape for joining paper when necessary.

For making up the garments you will need - a sewing machine (preferably with at least a basic zig-zag stitch), a good pair of scissors for cutting fabric (don't cut paper with your fabric shears as this will blunt the blades), machine threads to match your chosen fabric and buttons, pins and tailors chalk, an iron for pressing as well as pressing cloths and brown paper. I recommend brown paper because there is never the danger of leaving a water mark as there sometimes is with a damp cloth.

For a really professional finish a domestic overlock machine is worthwhile investing in. These machines range from a basic three thread for overcasting to a four or five thread machine for greater strength at the seam. The machine in figure 1 is a five thread model which overcasts and stitches a chain stitch seam in one operation. This is extremely useful for blouses and shirts.

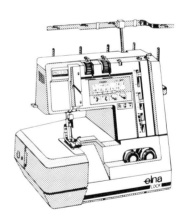

Figure 1

Pattern markings and abbreviations.

]	Place to fold.	↕	Straight grain on fabric.
><	Balance notches.	}	Gathers.
cb	Centre back.	np	Neck point
cf	Centre front.	sp	Shoulder point

Measurements

Before you begin to make your basic blouse pattern you will need
to take measurements. It is best to ask a friend to help here as
it is difficult to measure yourself. The blocks in the book are
constructed using metric measurements. Imperial equivalents are
best found on a metric/imperial tape measure. The measurements
you require to construct the blouse are - bust circumference,
waist circumference, hip circumference, nape to waist
measurement, sleeve length (from shoulder end to wrist) and elbow
length (from shoulder end to elbow). The shoulder width is not
easily defined and it is advisable to take the measurement
suggested in the instructions for the block construction, and
then check the finished measurement against your body. The chest
and cross back may be checked at the same time and adjustments
made if necessary. Ease for movement is added to the block
construction so it is best to take measurements wearing only
underwear. The blouse has 10cm of ease around the bust which is a
comfortable amount for this type of garment.

Make a note of your measurements here and proceed with the blouse
block construction and cut and sew the fashion you prefer.

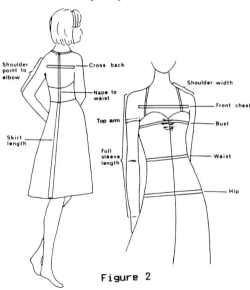

Nape to waist   cm.

Bust   cm.

Waist   cm.

Hip   cm.

Sleeve length   cm.

Elbow   cm.

Figure 2

6

BLOUSE/SHIRT BLOCK

The block is made on a rectangle made up of half the bust measurement plus ease by the length of the blouse. To construct this rectangle you will need a piece of paper measuring approximately 70cm by half the bust measurement plus 8cm.

The starting point is A which should be to the left hand edge of the paper and 4cm from the top edge.

A to B is the nape to waist measurement. This line is the centre back of the blouse block and future lines across the draft to the right must be at right angles to this centre back line.
  C is midway between A and B
  C to D is 2.5cm
  D to E is half the bust measurement plus 5cm ease.
(For bust sizes 104cm and above the ease will need to be 5.5cm)
Using lines A and B and lines D and E square across and up and down to form a rectangle measuring the nape to waist by half the bust plus ease. Mark the top intersection F and the lower intersection G. The line B to G is the waist line position and the line F to G is the centre front.
This completes the basic rectangle, figure 3.

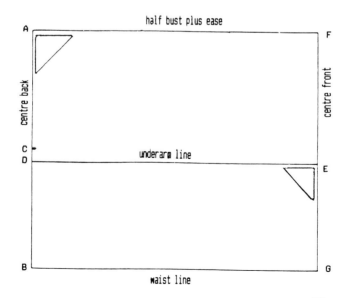

7

Figure 3

D to H is half D to E less 1cm.

Drop a vertical line from H to meet the waist line.

A to I is 7cm for sizes 90 to 100. For other sizes add 0.2cm for every 4cm bust increment and deduct 0.2cm for sizes 88 and below.

I to J is 2cm

Connect J to A with a suitable curve for the back neck. The back neck should be straight along the top line for about 3cm from A before the curve is shaped towards J.

Draw a line across the rectangle parallel to the top line but 1.5cm below it. This is the shoulder slope line.

For the purpose of the block draft it is advisable to use the shoulder width measurement from the table below that corresponds with your bust measurement. Any adjustments may be made before the blouse is traced onto pattern paper.

Bust	78-82	84-96	98-100	102-108	110-114
Shoulder	12	13	13.5	14	14.5

J to K is the shoulder width measurement plus 1cm ease. To find point K measure from J and bring the metre stick to rest on the shoulder slope line (14cm for size 92) Mark this temporary shoulder line with only a feint line or broken line as shown on the draft in figure 4.

Drop a vertical line from K to meet the line D to E (the underarm line)

L is midway A to C. Square across from L to meet the centre front line.

F to M is the same as A to I.

M to N is 2cm

N to O is the shoulder width plus 0.5cm. This is only a temporary line and should be marked with a feint or broken line. Drop a vertical line from O to meet the underarm line.

The armhole line may now be drawn in. As a guide follow the suggested measurements to help achieve a good shape. On the horizontal line from L to the centre front measure 0.5cm to the left of the vertical line from K for the back and 1.5cm to the right of the vertical line from O for the front.

Connect K to H with a curve as shown. This curve should cross the vertical line at a position of about 4cm from the underarm line and 2.5cm from the right angle. Now draw in the front armhole line from O to H. The curve should cross the vertical line at a position of about 2.5cm from the underarm line and 1.5cm from the right angle.

Note: these suggested measurements can only serve as a guide and personal variations will undoubtedly be necessary. Check the cross back measurement on the block with your body measurement and the front chest also and make adjustments where these are necessary.

The shoulder slope position now requires re-alignment, figure 4. Measure up from K to a point 1.5cm and redraw the shoulder line from this point to J making sure this new line is the same length as J to K. Extend the armhole to meet this new shoulder line. Now drop O by 1.5cm and redraw the line from N. The new shoulder line must measure the same as N to O. Adjust the armhole accordingly. This new position for the shoulder line allows for a straighter seam across the shoulder of a garment. The back shoulder seam is 0.5cm longer than the front and will require easing onto the front when making up. This allows just a little ease over the back shoulder.

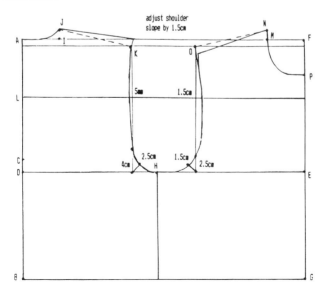

Figure 4

9

F to P is 6.5cm. Draw in the front neck curve from N to P. The front of the neck line should be flat for about 2cm from P to avoid the centre front coming to a point. Larger sizes may require a deeper neck line and should increase the measurement F to P to 7cm.

This completes the bodice part of the block outline above the waist but for a blouse extra length of approximately 20cm is required. To do this extend the centre back and centre front lines by 20cm.

B to Q is 20cm

G to R is 20cm. This is the hip level on an average figure. Connect Q to R.

Extend the line from H to meet the line Q to R.

The blouse block may be left completely straight without dart shaping but for some styles a little suppression by means of darts and seams is preferable.

Remember that the rectangle upon which the block is based is half the bust measurement plus 5cm ease for average sizes. The natural waist measurement is usually about 20cm less than the bust measurement, therefore, as only half a block is being constructed the suppression may be as much as 10cm at the waist area with this still leaving 5cm ease.

The front dart suppression is generally greater than the back. For a 10cm suppression the distribution should be 4cm for the front dart, 3cm for the back dart and 3cm at the side.

The position of the front dart is midway between the centre front and the front shoulder line (the vertical line from O). The apex of the dart is generally 6cm below the underarm line for average sizes, however this dart may need to be shorter for a fuller busted figure. The length of the dart below the waist is 8cm.

The position of the back dart is midway between the centre back and the shoulder line (the vertical line from K). The apex of the back dart should be 1.5cm below the underarm line and 12cm below the waist line. The side shaping of 3cm is taken out at the waist line and the apex is at H. The shaping below the waist crosses over at approximately 12cm below the waist line allowing a little extra width around the hip area. The back and front do overlap slightly now and must be traced off separately. Check that the overall measurement at the hip level is large enough to fit over your hips. If extra width is required this should be added at the side. Figure 5 shows the complete blouse block.

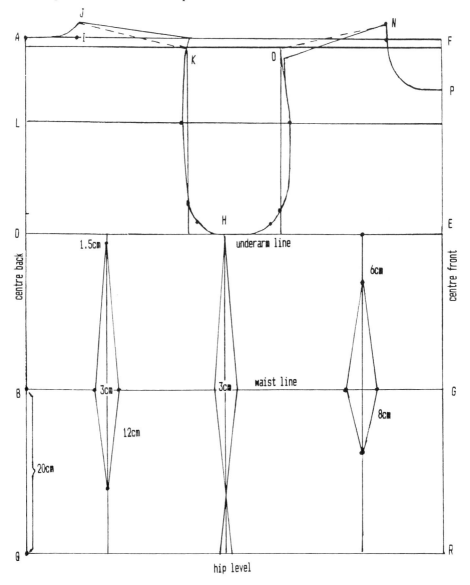

Figure 5

SLEEVE BLOCK

For the sleeve block you will require a piece of paper measuring your sleeve length plus 10cm by your top arm circumference plus 6cm.

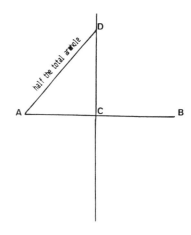

Figure 6

A to B is the top arm measurement plus 6cm. This line should be 30cm from the top of the paper. The top arm is measured around the fullest part of the arm between the elbow and shoulder.This measurement with the ease will be around 35 to 39cm on the average figure.

A to C is half A to B less 0.5cm. Draw a line up and down through C at right angles to the line A to B.

A to D is half the total armhole. (to measure the armhole on the blouse block hold the tape measure on its edge. This is the easiest way to measure a curve. Measure from K round through H to O) When you have the total measurement divide this in half. Starting with your metre stick at A on the sleeve block measure towards the vertical line for the distance of half the armhole measurement. This will give you the position for D, figure 6.

Connect D to B to form a "triangle". Note: This is not an exact triangle because C is not midway between A and B. Now divide the triangle into three sections between D and C. This need not be absolutely precise as it is only to serve as a guide to shaping the sleeve head. Divide the lower section in half again as shown with a broken line, figure 7.

Figure 7

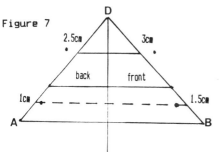

Figure 8

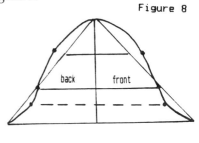

12

On the top line measure 2.5cm to the left of the triangle and mark a dot. Next measure 3cm to the right of the triangle on the top line and mark with a dot. Mark the left part of the triangle "Back" and the right part "Front" as shown in figure 7. At the position of the broken line measure 1cm to the right of the triangle for the back and mark this with a dot. Measure 1.5cm to the left of the triangle for the front section on the broken line.

Using the dots as a guide draw in the sleeve head curve from A to D and through to B. Note that the curved line crosses the triangle at the position of middle line. The sleeve head is now complete, figure 8.

To check that there is sufficient fullness in the sleeve head measure with the tape on edge. The sleeve head should be between 3cm to 5cm larger than the armhole. If necessary raise the crown slightly to ensure that there is this amount of fullness.

Figure 9 shows the full length sleeve.

D to E is the sleeve length. The sleeve length should be the arm measurement from the wrist to the end of the shoulder. (The end of shoulder is where the seam for a classic set-in sleeve would fit).

E to F is one third of A to B
E to G is the same as E to F
D to H is the elbow length. The elbow length is measured from shoulder end to elbow.

Connect A to F and B to G. Place square at H and draw a line to the left to meet the line A to F. Mark this I.

I to J is 1.5cm. Place the square at J on the line J to F and draw a line at right angles to meet line H to I. This forms the elbow dart.

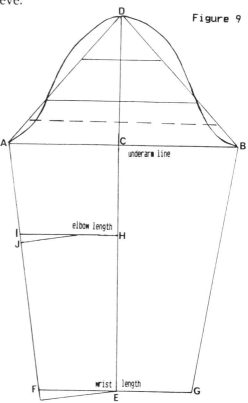

Figure 9

An elbow dart is rarely used but the back of the sleeve does need to be a little longer than the front to allow for comfortable movement.
The fullness can often be eased away rather than using a dart. Extend the back sleeve length at F by 1.5cm to allow for the dart to be taken out. Connect the extended line to E as shown on the sleeve block.

The sleeve head is slightly larger than the armhole. This allows for ease around the crown. To find the position for a balance notch in the crown of the sleeve you need to measure the blouse armhole. First measure the back armhole with the tape on edge from H to K raised. Now measure the same distance around the back of the sleevehead from A towards D and mark a dot. Measure the front armhole from H to O and record the same distance on the front sleevehead from B towards D and mark a dot. The correct crown height balance notch is midway between the two dots. This is the point to which the sleeve should match the shoulder seam.

Tracing the block

Having completed the draft of the blouse each piece must now be traced off onto card. To do this place the draft over the card and run the tracing wheel around the outline. This creates perforations on the card below and enables you to produce a fresh outline. Trace the back pattern first, then move the draft and trace off the front and so separating the two pattern pieces. Mark the underarm line. Trace off the sleeve in the same way.
Before you cut the pattern pieces out in the card it is advisable to check a couple of measurements to ensure that the blouse is going to fit around the shoulder area.
Measure your cross back and front chest and check that the blouse is larger than your body measurements by at least 1cm. Also check the shoulder width to ensure that this is neither too big or too small. (ask a friend to measure from the nape to the shoulder end on the body and check this measurement against the centre back to shoulder point on the draft) The shoulder will only require 1cm ease. Reshape the pattern if necessary, making the adjustment before cutting the card.

Seam and Hem Allowances and Facings.

Seam allowances are not included on the block but must be added
to the pattern before the blouse is cut. To do this take a copy
of the back and front and sleeve blocks and add seam allowances
all round except for the centre front, figure 11. The amount of
seam allowance is dependent upon the intended seam finish. Most
patterns allow 1.5cm and if you choose to follow this trend add
that amount of seam allowance. However, for the blouse you may
wish to use the overlock machine to neaten the raw edge and
stitch the seam in one operation as illustrated in figure 12. In
this case only the width of the machine setting will be necessary
for the seam allowance.

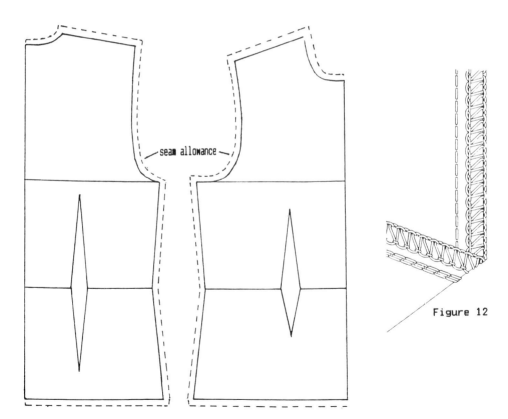

seam allowance

Figure 12

Figure 11

The blouse has a button clearance and a built on facing. To make the built on facing fold the paper to the right of the front pattern underneath the front as shown in figure 14, allowing 2cm for button clearance to the right of the centre front. Now measure 8cm from the fold and draw a broken line on the pattern from the hem to underarm line. From the underarm line curve the broken line to meet the shoulder line at 6cm from the neck point. Run along this line with your tracing wheel transferring the facing line to the paper below. Cut round the pattern piece with seam allowances. Open out the paper and cut along the perforated lines and the built-on facing is complete, figure 15.

Figure 15

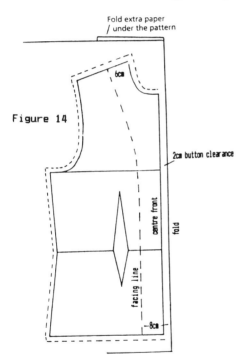

Fold extra paper / under the pattern

6cm

Figure 14

2cm button clearance

centre front

fold

facing line

—8cm—

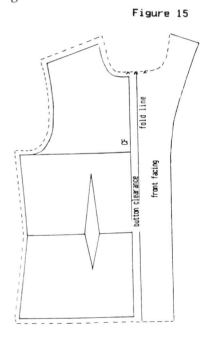

button clearance

front facing

fold line

For the back neck facing use the back block as a template and draw in the facing line as shown in figure 16. Trace off the back facing and indicate with a bracket that the centre back is to be placed to the fold.

back facing

facing line

MAKING UP THE BLOUSE

Cutting and marking the cloth.

Before you place the pattern pieces on the fabric it is advisable to iron out any creases and at the same time look for any flaws in the cloth. After ironing, fold the fabric with the selvedge edges together and lay the pattern pieces onto the double fabric. It is worth mentioning here that it is not a good policy to use the selvedge as part of the garment because the yarns used may be liable to shrinkage.

Pin the pattern to the cloth placing the centre back to the fold and the centre front towards the selvedge. If, for economical reasons you do find it necessary to reverse the pattern pieces be careful not to be caught out by thinking the fabric is the same both ways. Sometimes it is possible for what appears to be a plain fabric to shine a slightly different shade when turned the other way round. Jersey knit fabrics are particularly prone to this shading difference and I prefer to try and keep all my pattern pieces running the same way for the whole garment. Cut the fabric as close to the paper pattern as possible. Cut with even clear cuts holding your scissors with the flat edge running along the work surface. As each piece is cut place it to one side with the pattern piece still pinned in position for subsequent marking.

I prefer to use dressmakers tracing paper and a tracing wheel for markings. To use this place the waxed tracing paper between the pattern and the wrong side of the fabric. The coloured waxed side of the tracing paper should be next to the fabric. Full instructions are given on the tracing paper packet. Use the tracing wheel to mark the darts and balance notches. As soon as the blouse has been cut out it is a good idea to neaten the raw edges to prevent the cloth fraying. The best way to do this is by using an overlock machine which gives the most professional finish. Take care not to stretch the edges but guide the cloth under the machine without allowing it to drag.

If you do not have an overlock machine neaten the edge by using the zig-zag stitch on your sewing machine.

Darts

The darts must be correctly machine stitched to acquire a good finish. Fold the cloth along the centre line of the dart with the right sides together. Pin the darts in such a way that the dart markings meet. The pins should be arranged so that they cross the line for machining. To machine, place the blouse under the presser foot with the end of the dart in line with the needle and the main piece of the blouse to the left of the machine foot. Machine stitch the dart from one apex to the other removing the pins as you sew. At each apex work three or four stitches right on the fold and back stitch over these to finish off securely, figure 17.

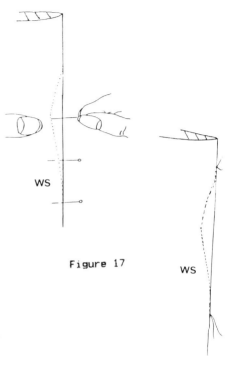

Figure 17

To make the blouse, first pin and machine the back and front shoulder seams with right sides together, figure 18a. Press the seam open, figure 18b, or if you have overlocked and stitched in one process press the seam towards the back of the blouse. The next step is the set in the sleeve.

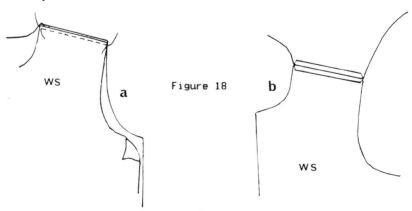

Figure 18

18

Set in sleeve

The generally accepted definition of a set in sleeve is one which is stitched into a garment around the natural armhole area of the bodice. The sleeve is always larger than the armhole to allow for fitting around the upper arm. The sleeve may be stitched to the blouse either on the flat with only the shoulder seam joined, or on the round where the sleeve and blouse seams have been previously stitched.

The **flat method** has gained great favour in the clothing industry and is frequently used for blouses and summer dresses. Pin and machine the shoulder seams of the blouse first with the right sides together. Pin the sleeve to the garment armhole area with the right sides together matching the crown of the sleeve with the shoulder seam. Pin at regular intervals easing away the fullness of the sleeve head. I do not like to use a gathering thread as suggested with so many commercial patterns. The aim of a nicely set sleeve is to stitch the sleeve with a smooth seam. No tucks should be in evidence on the sleeve. Ensure that the right sleeve is pinned into the right armhole and the left into the left. Machine these with the sleeve uppermost. Take in the correct seam allowance and ease the fabric under the presser foot. Flatten the sleeve head with your hands close to the presser foot, figure 19. It is surprisingly easy to ease away quite an amount of fabric without tucks by this method.

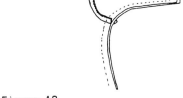

Figure 20

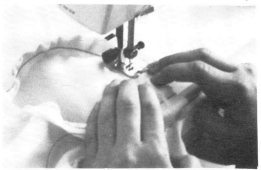

Figure 19

When the sleeve has been stitched to the armhole the side seam may be stitched. With right sides together, pin the side seams and the sleeve seams, matching the back and front sleeve seams, and machine stitch these together, figure 20. Neaten the raw edges together with zig zag stitch or overlock.

The **round method** is an
alternative way of making a set
in sleeve. Stitch the shoulder
seams and side seams of the
garment, figure 21. Machine the
underarm seam of the sleeve. A
wrist length sleeve will
necessitate the easing away of
the fullness around the elbow
area. A small dart is included
in the block at the elbow
position but I personally do
not care to use a dart and
advise against this because of
its rather ugly appearance.
Instead I ease away the
fullness allowed for the dart
over a distance of
approximately 8cm. This still
allows for the necessary
fullness around the back elbow area.

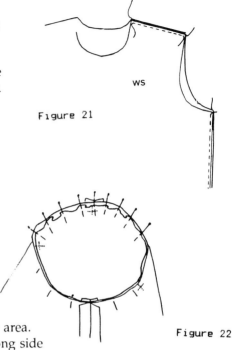

ws

Figure 21

Figure 22

Hold the garment with the wrong side
uppermost and pass the sleeve, with the right side out, through
the armhole. Pin the sleeve head to the shoulder seam with
right sides together.

Insert pins at the underarm seams to secure the sleeve to the
bodice. Be sure to have the correct sleeve in the correct side of
the garment. It is so easy to make mistakes especially when using
plain fabric. Do check that the back of the sleeve is pinned to
the back of the blouse. (It is helpful to mark a B with tailors
chalk on the wrong side of the fabric as soon as the pattern is
removed after cutting the cloth.) Pin at regular intervals from
the under arm position keeping the fabric flat for about a third
of the total armhole each side of the side seam. Then pin the
sleeve head distributing the ease evenly as shown in figure 22.
With the sleeve uppermost machine the sleeve into the armhole
taking the correct seam allowance. Flatten the sleeve head with
your hands close to the presser foot to ensure that no tucks are
made. Press the seam open initially to obtain a good line, then
press the seam towards the sleeve.

Figure 23

Facing the Round Neck.

With right sides together pin and machine stitch the back neck facing to the front facing at the shoulder position. Fold back the built on facing bringing right sides together and matching the centre fronts. Pin into position around the neck and machine stitch all round the neck stitching front and back facings onto the blouse, figure 24.

Turn the facings to the inside of the blouse and press ensuring that the seam is on the inside. The facing should not show on the right side of the garment. Hold the facing in place by stitching in the channel along the shoulder line, figure 25.

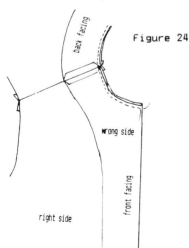

Figure 24

back facing

wrong side

front facing

right side

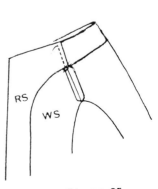

RS

WS

Figure 25

Buttonholes.

Before making the button holes you must mark the position of these with tailors chalk onto the right front of the blouse. Remember that the shanks or fish eye will rest at the end of the buttonhole which is nearest to the edge of the blouse, and that when the button is fastened there should be some clearance between the button and the front edge of the garment. Don't guess at the buttonhole positions-work them out with the aid of a tape measure. The buttonhole needs to be positioned almost the same distance from the front edge of the blouse as the diameter of the intended button. This will ensure that when the button is fastened half the button will overlap the buttonhole and there will be a clearance the size of half a button. This achieves a good balance. The length of the buttonhole needs to be the size of the button plus an allowance for ease of fastening. The ease allowance will vary according to the thickness of the button. Generally an allowance of 0.2cm should be sufficient but for thicker buttons it is advisable to allow a little more.

A machine made buttonhole has two parallel rows of satin stitch and a bar tack at each end. The buttonhole is worked prior to the cut being made between the two rows of satin stitch. Your sewing machine manual will give details of how to work the buttonhole.

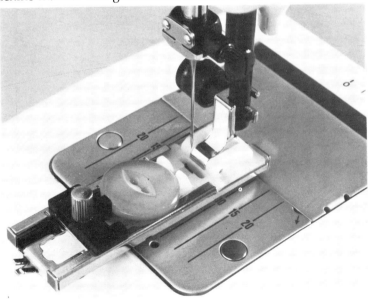

Figure 26

There are various attachments available to help you achieve really superb buttonholes. Some of the attachments fit onto the buttonhole foot and are supplied with the machine while others are offered as optional extras. The measuring device shown in figure 26 is extremely useful in that it may be set to the size of the button and has allowance for ease included. Once set to the correct size the button is removed and the guide is there to ensure that all the buttonholes are the same size.

Hem

The blouse is now complete except for the hem at the lower edge and the sleeve. There are several hemming methods and the way in which you finish your hem will depend to a large extent on the sewing machine you are using. You may choose to overlock the raw edge and then top stitch the hem or zig-zig stitch and top stitch. One hem finish which I feel is very under-used is the scroll hemmer. The hemmer foot guides the fabric through a scroll turning the raw edge in and making a finished hem about (0.5cm) wide, figure 27.

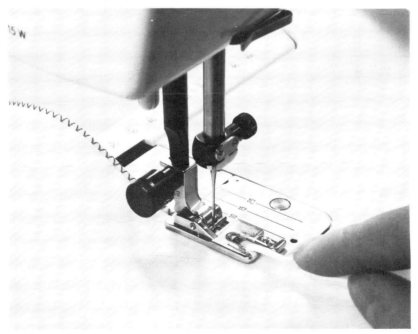

Figure 27

23

NECKLINES

The finish of the neck line plays an important part in the design of a garment and may be cut to almost any shape. A different neckline can completely transform a garment into a new style with so little effort.

A built on facing is preferable for most shapes, therefore you will need paper large enough to accommodate the blouse front pattern plus about 20cm to the right of the centre front. Draw round the block pattern, add the button clearance and mark the facing line as shown in figure 30. Fold the paper that is to the right underneath the block outline and you are now ready to draw in the desired shape for the neckline. This procedure is the same for the four styles that follow.

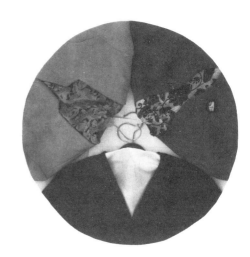

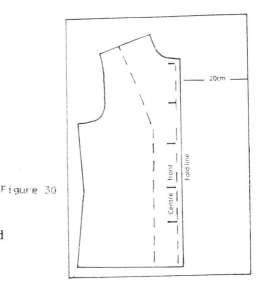

Figure 30

A Square Neckline.

Having prepared the paper and folded the extra paper under the pattern draw in the new neck shape, figure 31. Be careful not to make this too large. Remember it is always possible to adapt this to a larger square after it is cut but it is difficult to rectify

the situation if reversed. You will see that I have suggested widening the neck at the shoulder by only 3cm. The depth and width at the centre front is really a matter of personal choice but do consider the underwear you intend to wear with the garment. Straps showing from underwear will most certainly spoil the effect and your efforts in making the garment will be wasted. Remember the cross over point at the front will be the centre front line, therefore the width measurement should be from this point. Now trace the new outline and trace along the facing line. Transferring the shape to the paper underneath.

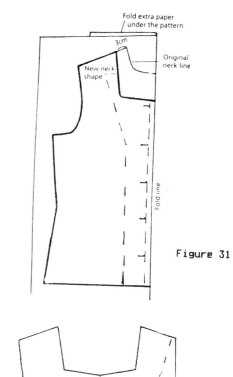

Figure 31

Open out the pattern and cut away the surplus paper, figure 32. Remember to add seam allowances to complete the pattern.

Sweet-heart Neckline

For the sweet-heart neckline follow the same procedure as for the square neck but instead of the "square" being almost at right angles to the centre front draw a slanted line which dips a little more at the front as shown with a broken line in

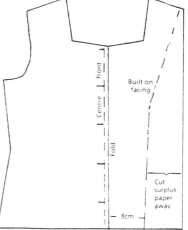

Figure 32

25

figure 33. Using the broken lines as a guide draw in the new outline curving away from the broken line as shown. The suggested measurements are given only as a guide to help you draw the sweet-heart shape and may be adjusted to your own personal choice. Trace off the new neckline, open the pattern and trim off the excess paper as described before, figure 34. Remember to add seam allowances to complete the pattern.

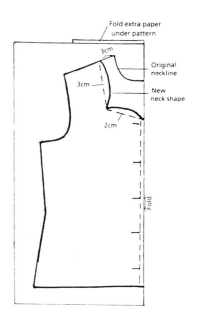

Figure 33

The V Neckline

Prepare the paper as before with the facing allowance folded under the pattern. Draw on the V neck shape as shown in figure 35.
Trace the new outline and the facing line. Open the pattern, cut away excess and add seam allowances, figure 36.

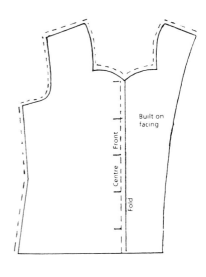

Figure 34

26

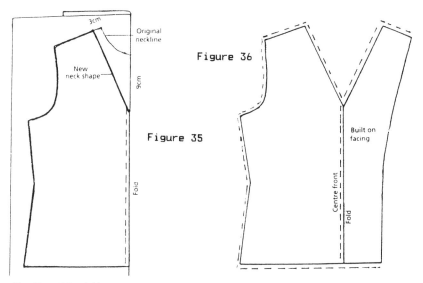

Figure 36

Figure 35

Scallop Neckline

The V neckline may be easily adapted to make the pretty scallop neckline. First prepare the paper as before and draw in the V neck as shown with a broken line. Draw in the two curved lines to give the scalloped effect, figure 37. The measurements are given to help achieve the desired shape but these may be adjusted to personal taste. Trace the new outline and the facing line and open out the paper, figure 38. Trim off the excess paper from the facing and add seam allowances to complete the pattern.

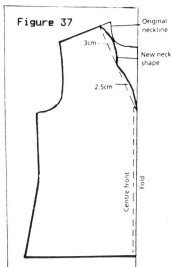

Figure 37

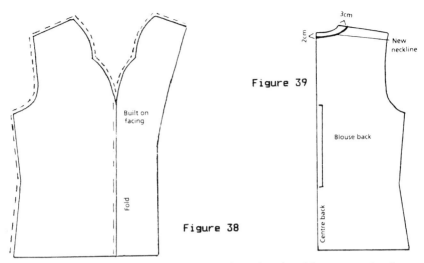

Built on facing

Fold

Figure 38

3cm

2cm

New neckline

Figure 39

Blouse back

Centre back

Because the neckline has been widened at the shoulder a new back pattern will need to be cut to correspond with the front. To make the back pattern draw round the block and widen the neck at the shoulder by 3cm or whatever the amount you chose to widen the front, as shown in figure 39. The neckline has been lowered by 2cm in figure 39 but this is only a suggestion. The shape of the back neck may be round, square, V or indeed any shape you care to choose provided a facing is cut for the same shape.

Trace off the new shape and draw in a facing line making this the same width at the shoulder as the front facing, figure 40.

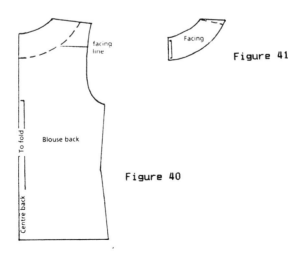

facing line

Facing

Figure 41

To fold

Blouse back

Centre back

Figure 40

Trace off the back facing and reshape the shoulder line by taking 1cm off the inside edge as shown with a broken line in figure 41. If this amount is not taken off the facing does not lie flat inside the garment when it is made up. Indicate with a bracket that the centre back is to the fold and add seam allowances to the back pattern and the back facing to complete the pieces.

To make up the various shaped necklines first machine the shoulder seams of the garment with right sides together. Next join the facings at the shoulder with right sides together. Then fold back the front facing with the right sides together and machine stitch round the new shaped neckline as shown in figure 42. Turn the facing to the inside of the garment and press the seam towards the inside in such a way that it is not visible from the right side. Carefully snip into the corners of the shapes to enable the cloth to lie flat when turned. It is sometimes beneficial to press the facing seam open first and then press the seam towards the inside of the garment to achieve a good finish.

To cut an interfacing for any of the suggested shapes you will need to take a copy of the facing piece of the pattern. This is the piece to the right of the fold which should be traced off and separated by cutting along the fold line. Choose an interfacing suitable for your fabric and iron this onto the facing before stitching the shoulder seams.

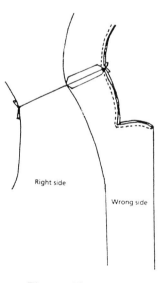

Right side

Wrong side

Figure 42

29

COLLARS.

When a collar is used by a dress designer, it is usually intended that this feature should be a focal point of the garment. Many women have personal reasons for preferring a collar - to disguise a long thin neck, to hide tell-tale age lines, to detract from broad shoulders or for extra warmth around the throat, to name but a few.

The shapes and type of collars change frequently according to fashion trends, but the main principles and cutting techniques remain the same. The inner edge of the collar, which is sewn to the neck edge of the garment must measure the same as the neck line of the bodice. However, this inner edge need not necessarily be the same shape as the neck outline. The shape of the outer edge determines the set of the collar and the amount of roll. This outer edge is called the fall edge. If the fall edge fits around the body area, laying flat over the back, shoulder and front of the body, this is a flat collar. However, if the outer circumference of the collar is shortened, tightening the fall edge around the body, the collar will be forced to a new level, and an amount of stand or roll will be created at the neck area.

Before constructing a collar, adjust the neck line of the bodice to accommodate a collar. The amount of adjustment is dependent upon the type of collar and whether it is intended to fit close to the neck or stand away. The bodice is cut to fit comfortably around the base of the neck, therefore for a flat collar or close-fitting collar it should only be necessary to drop the centre front by about 1cm and take off approximately 0.5cm at the neck point, the centre back remaining unchanged. For a stand-away collar 2 to 3cm may be taken off at the neck-point, and the line may be reshaped accordingly.

Flat Collar

To construct a flat collar, place the back and front blouse blocks together at the neck point. Overlap the shoulder line at the shoulder point by 3cm. If this amount is not taken out the collar will not lie flat against the body in wear. Lower the neck edge of the collar by 1cm at the centre front to achieve a better shape. Decide upon the desired depth of the collar, and measure guide lines from the neck edge as shown (8cm in this example). Draw in the fall edge of the collar as shown by the broken line, figure 43, and mark a notch at the shoulder position. Mark the centre back on the collar piece. Trace off this collar, figure 44, and to achieve a rolled effect cut the collar from the fall edge to within 0.2cm of the neck edge in four places. Overlap each of these cut lines by 2cm to shorten the fall edge, figure 45. Place the centre back to a folded piece of paper and redraw this new shape record the notches and add seam allowances. Cut out the complete collar as shown in figure 46.

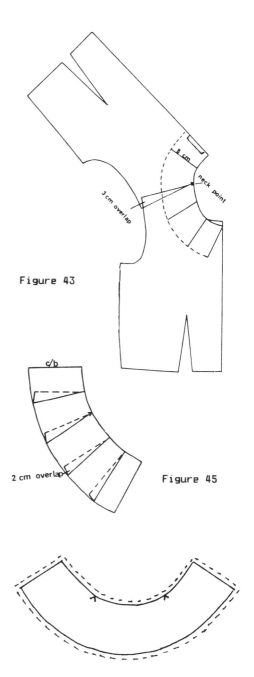

Figure 43

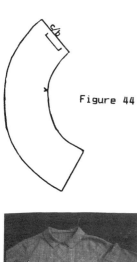

Figure 44

Figure 45

Figure 46

The flat collar may be stitched onto the neckline using the front facing to neaten the front neck edge. The back neck edge may be finished with overlock or zig-zag stitch avoiding the use of a back neck facing. Facings do tend to be bulky and I do try to avoid using them whenever possible.

If necessary iron on a light weight interfacing to the under collar. Pin the collar with the right sides together and machine round the outer edge of the collar. At the corners of the collar it is best to make one or two stitches in a diagonal direction to achieve a smooth seam when turning the collar, figure 47. Trim excess fabric from the seams. Turn and press the collar with the seam towards the under-side making it invisible on the top collar. Find the centre back of the collar and the centre back of the garment and pin the collar into position with the right sides of the garment to the right side of the under collar. Work from the centre back round to the left and right fronts pinning the collar into position at the same time matching the notches to the shoulder seam and centre front.

Now machine stitch the collar into position, stitching in the centre of the seam allowance, figure 48. Fold the front facing back matching the centre front notches enclosing the front collar between the garment and the facing, figure 49.

The right side of the facing should be to the right side of the garment. Pin and machine the facing to the garment securing the collar in place. Take the correct seam allowance and machine all round the neck edge from left front to right front.

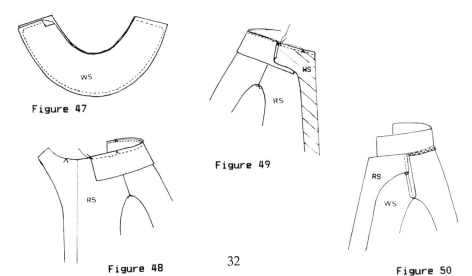

Figure 47

Figure 48

Figure 49

Figure 50

32

Turn the facing and turn a small hem across the shoulder area.
Machine this to the shoulder seam along the channel of machine
stitching. Neaten the back neck edge with zig zag stitch or
overlock, figure 50.

One piece collar.

To construct the one piece collar you will need a piece of paper
measuring the total neck size plus 5cm by 18cm.
Fold the paper in half lengthways and then in half so that the
folds come together. Place the folded paper on the table in
front of you with the lengthways fold at the top. Mark the top
left-hand corner A,figure 51.

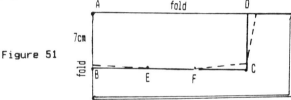

Figure 51

Measure down from A to B = 7cm.
B to C is half the neck size. Using the set square form a
rectangle and mark the top right-hand corner D. Measure from
centre back to the shoulder on the blouse block. Now measure the
same distance from B along the bottom of the rectangle and mark
this E. F is midway between E and C.
Now raise B by 0.2cm and redraw the line to E as shown with a
broken line. Raise C by 0.75cm and redraw this line to F as
shown. Adjust the position of D by 0.5cm as shown with broken
line. The broken lines are the correct shape for the collar.
The collar may now be cut out adding the seam allowances at the
same time. To assist in keeping the folded paper in place whilst
you are cutting it is helpful to use paper clips. After cutting,
open the pattern and mark the balance notches at E. Redraw and
add seam allowances, figure 52.

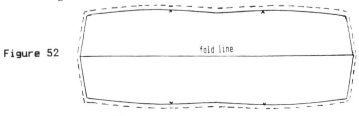

Figure 52

33

To make the collar fold the fabric along the fold line with
right sides together and stitch each end. Then turn the collar
right side out and press the seams. Machine the shoulder seams
of the garment and stitch the collar to the neck edge matching
the notches at the shoulder seams. Bring the garment facing back
over the collar as described in figure 49 and stitch the facing
in place enclosing the collar. Turn the facing to the inside of
the garment and press. I do not always find it necessary to use
an interfacing in this collar but if one is used it is advisable
to iron this on only half of the collar. To cut the interfacing
fold the pattern in half lengthways and use this outline for the
pattern. Iron the interfacing on to the wrong side and after
stitching the ends make sure that the interfaced piece of the
collar is the under collar and that this is the piece stitched
next to the garment.This
collar may be worn close
to the neck or open.

Shirt Collar.

To cut a shirt collar, draw a rectangle measuring half the total
neck line plus 2cm clearance by 3cm. Shape the front edge with a
curve as shown with a broken line and divide the rectangle into
three sections as shown, figure 53. Mark a balance notch 2cm from
the front (right hand side) to indicate that this is the centre
front. Cut this out and cut each line almost through to enable
you to overlap the cuts by 0.5cm each as shown in figure 54.
Redraw the new shape and draw in the shape of the collar as

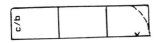

Figure 53

overlap 5mm

Figure 54

illustrated with a broken line in figure 55. This is the fall of
the collar. The front edge of the fall should cross the neck edge
of the stand at the button clearance i.e. 2cm from the end. Fold
the paper from above the outline underneath the collar as shown
in figure 56. The fold of the paper should be 0.75cm clear of the
centre back as shown.

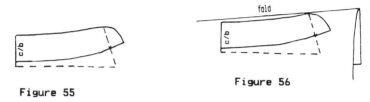

Figure 55

Figure 56

Use your tracing wheel to trace the broken line through to the
underneath paper. Open out the paper and cut along the
perforations outlining the collar fall. Cut along the line of the
stand and the front curved button clearance. Place the pattern
piece against a folded piece of paper as shown in figure 57, add
seam allowances and cut this out. Open out the paper and your
shirt collar is complete, figure 58. A top collar and under
collar will be required, therefore the collar should be cut on
double thickness fabric.

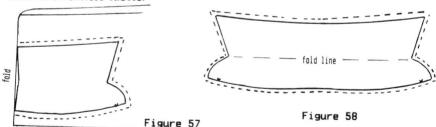

Figure 57

Figure 58

Use an interlining if necessary and make the collar in the same
way as described for a flat collar. Pin top and under collar with
right sides together and machine stitch all round the fall edge
from the right front to the left. Leave the neck edge open. Turn
the collar right side out and press. Find the centre back of the
collar and the centre back of the blouse and pin the two together
with the under collar against the blouse, figure 59. Pin the
collar in position matching the notches to the centre front.
Stitch the collar onto the blouse. Now fold the facing back over
the collar and machine stitch this, enclosing the collar between

the facing and the blouse front in the same way as described for the flat collar. Now turn the facing to the inside of the blouse and stitch along the shoulder seam and overlock the back seam in just the same way as for a flat collar, figure 60.

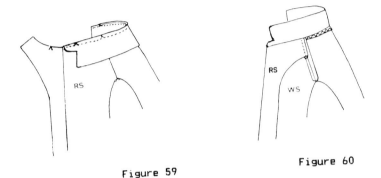

Figure 59

Figure 60

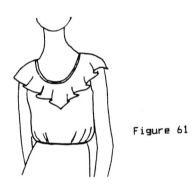

Figure 61

Flounced Collar

This flounced collar is cut wide enough to fall over the shoulder making a cap sleeve as well as a collar.

The first step is the widen the neckline of the blouse to the desired shape. As the new neckline will be large enough to pass over the head a front opening will not be necessary and the centre front may be placed to the fold of the fabric when cutting out. Be careful not to cut the neckline too large.

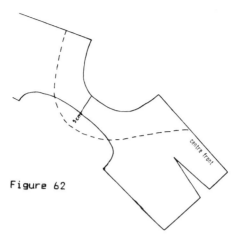

Figure 62

Now place the back and front shoulders together and draw in the collar shape as shown with a broken line in figure 62. The collar extends beyond the shoulder point by approximately 5cm in the example illustrated.

Trace off the collar, mark the centre front and centre back and the shoulder line. Cut from the fall edge to within 0.2cm of the neck edge at regular intervals (8 times). Spread the collar round into a circle as shown in figure 63a.

To avoid a seam at the centre front and centre back of the collar where it would be very conspicuous divide the collar in two at the shoulder seam and then add seam allowances, figure 63b. The centre front and centre back may be placed to the fold of the fabric when cutting out.

Figure 63

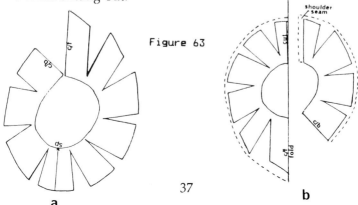

37

a   b

Only a fairly fine fabric should be used for the collar which may be double with a seam around the fall edge or a single fabric may be used and hemmed or finished by overlock satin stitch.

The suggested neck edge illustrated in figure 61 is a bound edge. The bound neckline requires a strip of fabric cut on the bias about 2cm wide. To find the true bias, turn over a corner of the fabric so that the warp and weft threads run parallel to each other, figure 64a. Cut along the fold and cut the required strips parallel to this first cut. If it is necessary to make a join in the strips, pin these with right sides together and stitch on the straight grain figure 64b, press the seam open and trim off edges (figure 64c). Always try to avoid using a joined strip on the front of the blouse.

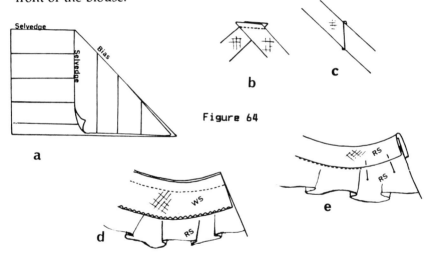

Figure 64

Neaten one edge of the strip by zig-zag or overlock. Stitch the flounced collar to the neck edge of the blouse and then stitch the bias strip with the right side of the strip to the right side of the collar, figure 64d.

Now press the binding towards the neckline. Pin the neatened edge so that it overlaps the seam line. Pin from the right side. Now top stitch from the right side, stitching as close to the edge of the binding as possible with a matching thread, figure 64e. The stitching becomes inconspicuous as the binding rolls back over this in wear.

Revers

A rever is part of the blouse front which is usually faced and turned back along the crease line. The shape and size of the rever varies according to vogue, but, as with collars, the construction techniques change very little.

Figure 65

To cut the pattern for the style, figure 65, draw around the front blouse block. Adjust the neck line to a V front and draw in the button clearance. As this is a double breasted garment an allowance of 6cm is made to the right of the centre front as shown in figure 66.

Draw in the shape required for the rever. Mark the crease line along the V front. Have sufficient paper on the right-hand side to fold along the crease line underneath the drawn rever outline, figure 67.

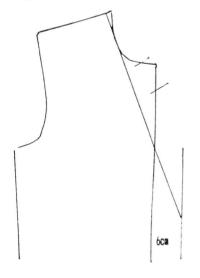

6cm

Figure 66

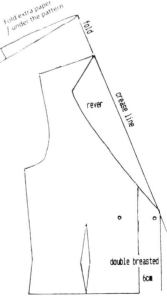

Fold extra paper under the pattern

fold

rever

crease line

double breasted

6cm

Figure 67

Trace off the rever shape, transferring the rever to the right-hand side as shown in figure 68. Add seam allowances to complete the pattern piece.

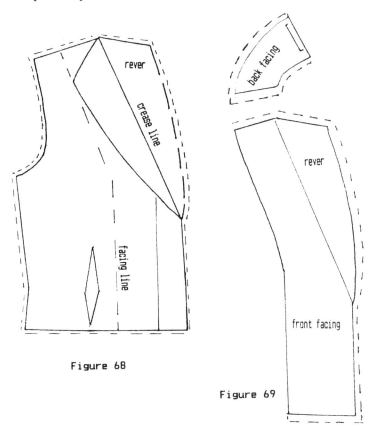

Figure 68

Figure 69

This rever, which is built onto the garment will form the under part when it is folded back. A top rever should now be cut together with the facing. To do this, mark the facing edge and trace off the rever and facing in the usual way, figure 69. Record the crease line on the top rever and facing piece.

To make the rever, first machine stitch the shoulder seams with right sides together, figure 70. Join the back and front facings with right sides together at the shoulder, figure 71.

Now, matching shoulder seams, pin and stitch the facing to the garment all round the front and back neck edge with right sides together, figure 72. Turn the facings to the inside of the garment, figure 72a. Finally fold back the rever to the right side of the garment and press carefully with brown paper between rever collar and iron to prevent any marking on the fabric.

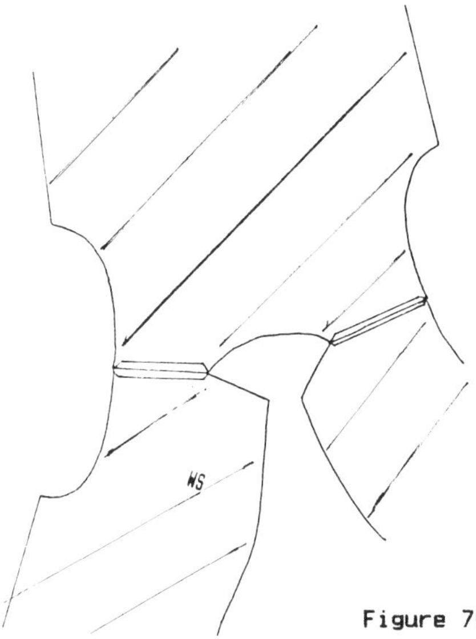

Figure 70

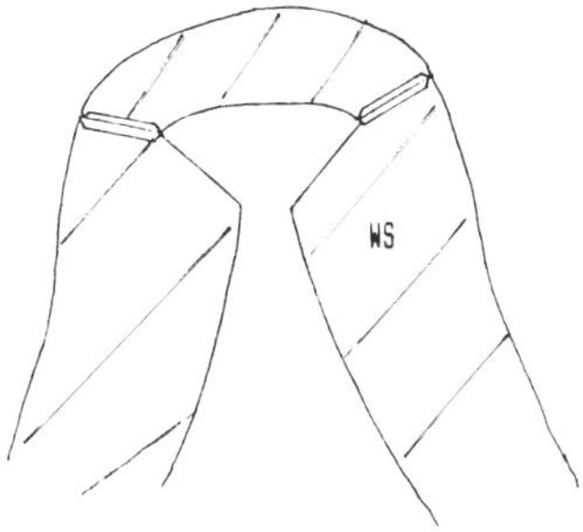

Figure 71

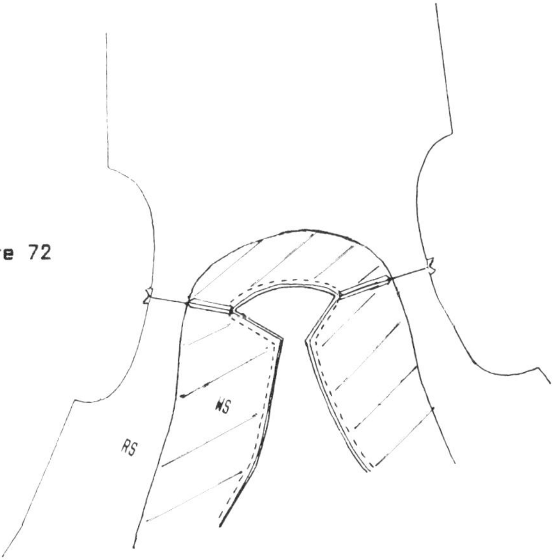

Figure 72

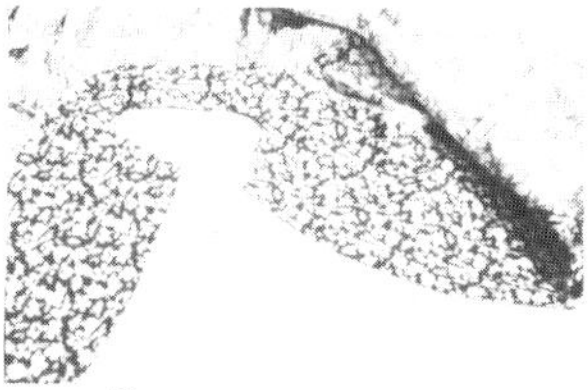

a

41

SLEEVES

By simply changing the style of the sleeves the plain blouse can
be completely transformed into a garment suitable for any
occasion.

Long Full Sleeve

This sleeve has fullness at
the crown, and at the wrist
the fullness is gathered
into the cuff.

Draw around the full-length sleeve block and cut this out.
Connect the underarm points with a straight line, and divide the
sleeve head into four sections, figure 74.
Cut down from the crown height to the underarm line, and cut
along this line to within 0.2cm of the underarm points. Cut the
remaining two lines from the sleeve head towards the horizontally
cut line, Spread the crown as illustrated and redraw the outline,
figure 75.
Shorten the sleeve to allow for the cuff. Draw a line vertically
from the crown height to the wrist line. Decide upon the width
required to be gathered into the cuff (approximately 40cm).

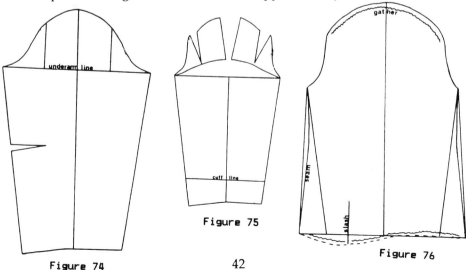

Figure 74

Figure 75

Figure 76

42

Divide this width equally either side of the vertical line and extend the wrist line accordingly. Connect the underarm points to the ends of this lower line with a guide line. To avoid excessive fullness at the upper arm position, reshape the seam as suggested with a curved line. Reshape the lower edge of the sleeve by lengthening the back part by approximately 2cm to allow for contour, figure 76. Mark the position for an opening and add seam allowances to finish the pattern piece.

The cuff pattern is a rectangle measuring twice the depth of the required cuff by the length of the wrist circumference plus ease and overlap allowances.

Puff and Tulip Sleeve

Draw round the sleeve block shortening this to the desired length. The length may vary according to fashion trends. Draw in the centre line and a line each side. These lines should cover approximately one third of the width of the sleeve, figure 77.

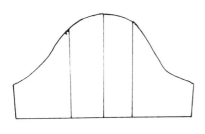

Figure 77

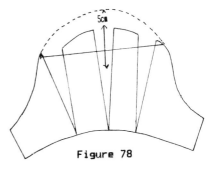

Figure 78

Cut out the sleeve and cut down each line from the sleeve head to within 0.2cm of the sleeve edge. Spread the sleeve head, opening each cut by approximately 4cm to 6cm. To achieve a raised crown the line must be raised by approximately 5cm at the centre shaping this into the sleeve head as shown by a broken line in figure 78. To make this up into a puff sleeve gather the sleeve head back to the original size and fit into the armhole in the usual way.

To make the sleeve puff up and look like a puff sleeve rather than a badly set in sleeve it is advisable to stiffen the crown with either self fabric or fine net. To make a pattern for the stiffening draw a line across the finished pattern piece at the raised crown area as shown in figure 78.

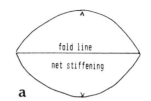

a

Place the line on a folded piece of paper and outline the sleeve head above the line. Cut this out and open as shown in figure 78a.

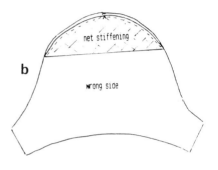

b

Stitch the folded stiffening to the sleeve head before gathering and stitching into the armhole, figure 78b.

Tulip Sleeve

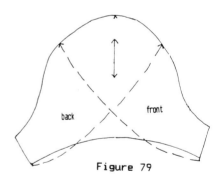

Figure 79

To create the tulip sleeve follow the same procedure as described for the puff sleeve. Draw the shape for the tulip. A guide to the position of the shaping is to divide the sleeve head into thirds as well as the lower edge of the sleeve. Draw curved lines from the sleeve head through the lower edge of the sleeve and round to the underarm edge as shown in figure 79.

Mark balance notches, grain line and back and front. Trace off each piece recording the markings. Add seam allowances to each piece, figure 80.

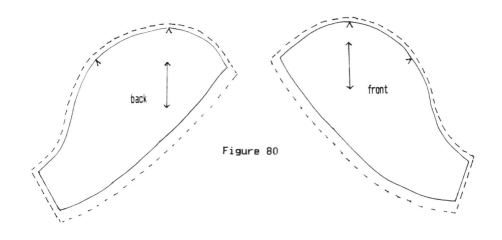

back

front

Figure 80

To make up, hem the curved line and press. The hem may be made by using the scroll hemmer foot or it may be overlocked and top stitched. Lay the back over the front with right sides uppermost, match the centre notch and bring the hemmed edge of the back over the front to meet at the notch. Run a machine stitched gathering thread through the two layers of fabric at the crown. Pull up the gathers to measure the same as the original block. Fit into the armhole in the usual way, figure 81.

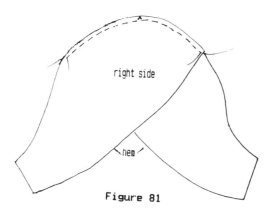

right side

hem

Figure 81

45

Flared Short Sleeve

This sleeve is flared at the
hem but fits into the armhole
without gathers.

Take a copy of the sleeve block
cut to the desired length.
Divide the sleeve into four
sections by drawing three lines
from the sleeve head to the
lower edge as illustrated 82.

Cut each line from the lower edge to within 0.2cm of the sleeve
head. Place this on a clean piece of paper and spread the lower
edge evenly adding the flare required (approximately 8 to 10cm)
Copy the outline and add seam allowances to complete the pattern.
Note that although the sleeve head shape has been changed, this
still measures the same as the block. When it is sewn into the
armhole the lower part will hang in gentle flounces, figure 83.

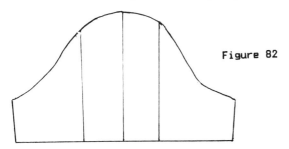

Figure 82

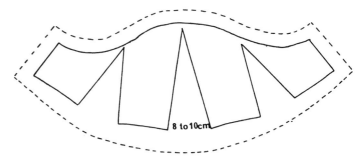

8 to 10cm

Figure 83

Sleeve with Contrast Panel

This sleeve with a contrast panel adds interest to a dress and jacket when the contrast fabric is the same as the dress.

Draw round the sleeve shortening this to the desired length. Draw in the shape of the contrast "V". The size of the contrast panel is a matter of personal choice but for a guide the width at the crown area may be approximately one third of the total sleeve head. The apex of the "V" may be a little lower than the underarm line, figure 84.

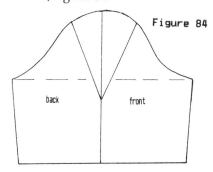

Figure 84

back   front

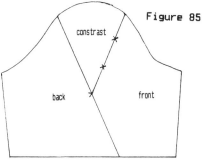

Figure 85

contrast

back   front

Mark each section, back, front and contrast respectively and extend the back line beyond the apex to meet the sleeve edge, figure 85. Mark two balance notches on the front side of the "V" and one at the apex.

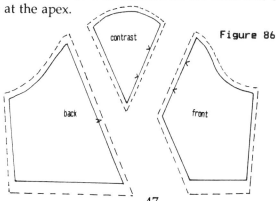

Figure 86

contrast

back   front

Trace off each section, add seam allowances and record balance notches, figure 86.

To make up the sleeve stitch the contrast to the front section with right sides together and matching the notches. Press the seams open, figure 87.

Next stitch the front to the back with right sides together, figure 88. Press the seams flat and set the sleeve into the armhole in the usual way.

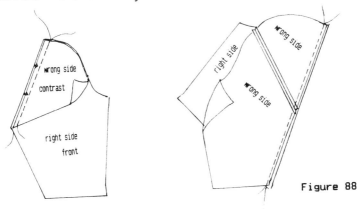

Figure 87

Figure 88

Short Sleeve with Turn Up Cuff

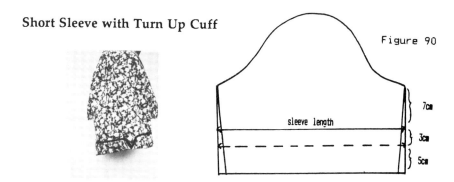

Figure 90

7cm
3cm
5cm

sleeve length

Draw round the sleeve and shorten to the desired length which is 7cm along the underarm line in figure 90. Add the depth of the cuff to the lower part of the sleeve - 3cm this is the fold line as shown by a broken line. Then add the hem allowance which should be 2cm greater than the cuff allowance - 5cm in figure 90. Add seam allowances to complete the pattern piece.

To make up the sleeve first stitch the underarm seams. Then fold along the fold line (broken line) bringing right sides together and stitch a V shape in the centre of the sleeve. The apex of the V should be 3cm from the fold, figure 91.

Cut out the V and turn the hem allowance to the inside of the sleeve, making a facing to the V and to the edge of the sleeve. Top stitch the hem into position, figure 92.
Finally turn back the turn up onto the right side of the sleeve and press into position, figure 93.

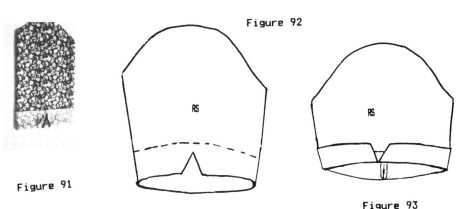

Figure 92

RS

RS

Figure 91

Figure 93

49

Pleated Sleeve

For a pleated sleeve it is best to fold the pleat in the paper
before taking a copy of the sleeve. To do this draw 5 vertical
lines measuring the sleeve length. The pleats in the picture are
3cm wide so draw the lines 3cm apart. Then fold the outer lines
to meet the centre line. Place the sleeve block over the folded
paper and draw round as shown in figure 94.

Cut the pattern out and open up the pleats. Mark notches at the
top and bottom of the sleeve on the outer lines to indicate the
pleat lines. Add seam allowances to complete the pattern piece,
figure 95.

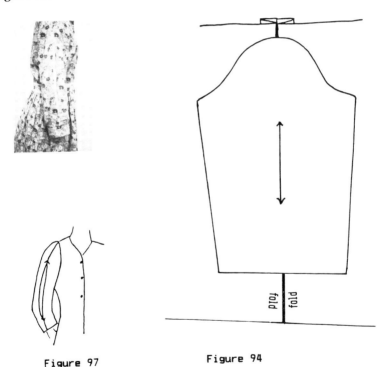

Figure 97   Figure 94

To make up, first fold the sleeve along the centre line matching
the balance notches as in figure 96. Machine stitch for about
12cm from the top notch down the sleeve at the pleat position and
stitch about 6cm from the wrist as shown.

50

Open out the sleeve and press the pleat into position. Arrows may be top stitched to hold the underpleat in position. Join the underarm seam and set into the armhole in the usual way, figure 97.

If you wish to use a contrast fabric for the underpleat the two centre sections must be separated from the sides and seams need to be allowed. The underpleat may then be cut in a contrast fabric.

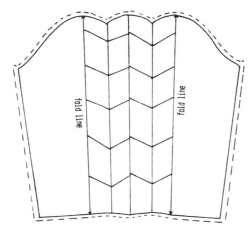

Figure 95

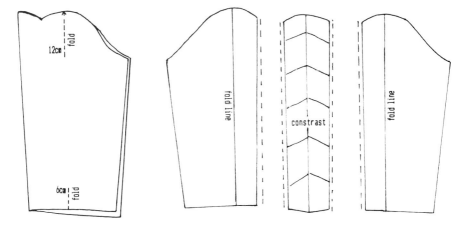

Figure 96   Figure 98

51

THE PRINCESS LINE AND WING SEAM.

The original blouse block is cut with a generous amount of ease. However, there are styles that require a more fitted bodice. For this a greater amount will need to be taken up in dart suppression. To have a garment fitting at the waist you need to measure your own waist and halve this. Then measure the block excluding the darts. Remember the block is only half a garment. The difference will need to be taken out by means of larger darts as shown in figure 99 but you still need to allow a little ease of 1cm or 2cm on half the garment. The new dart is drawn with a broken line. Note that for this adaptation the block is cut only to the waist.

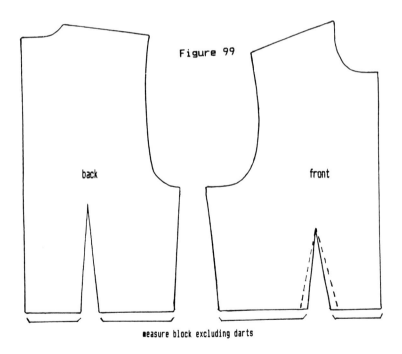

Figure 99

back

front

measure block excluding darts

The Princess Line and Wing Seam styles have the shaping in the front of the garment therefore the larger dart suppression is taken out at the front.

For the **Princess Line** take a copy of the block with the enlarged dart. Draw the style line from the shoulder to the apex of the dart as shown with a broken line in figure 100.

Cut this out and cut down the style line from the shoulder to within 0.2cm of the apex of the dart. Cut out the dart taking care not to cut the pattern right through. Now close the dart slightly and in so doing open up a dart in the shoulder area as shown in figure 101.

Redraw the pattern and shorten the new shoulder dart as shown by broken line. Mark notches at the apex of the darts. The apex of the darts should be about 12cm apart. Mark a grain line parallel with the centre front.

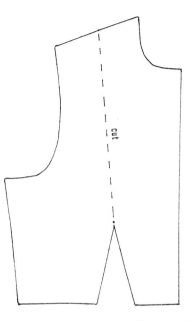

Figure 100

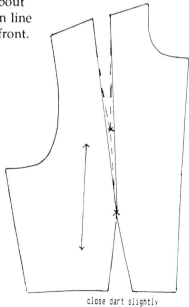

close dart slightly

53

Figure 101

Separate the two panels by cutting out the darts and cutting along the broken line. Redraw each piece and add seam allowances. The button clearance and facing should also be built on to the pattern. The pattern should be lengthened to blouse or jacket length to complete the pattern. To do this add the desired length and shape the style lines outwards to accommodate the hips. Check the size of the pattern against the size of the hips to make sure enough shaping has been allowed and make adjustments if necessary, figure 102.

The back block must of course be lengthened to correspond with the front and a seam may be cut right through the back to match the front, figure 103.

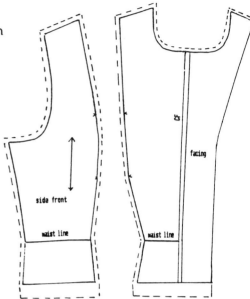

Figure 102

Princess Line Dress

The blouse pattern for the Princess Line can be easily adapted to make a pattern for a dress. Measure down from the waist line on the pattern for the desired skirt length. Extend the style lines to the desired length adding some extra width at the hem as shown in figure 105. The extra width at the hem may be as full as you wish and the 6cm given in figure 105 is only a suggestion.

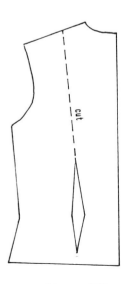

Figure 103

54

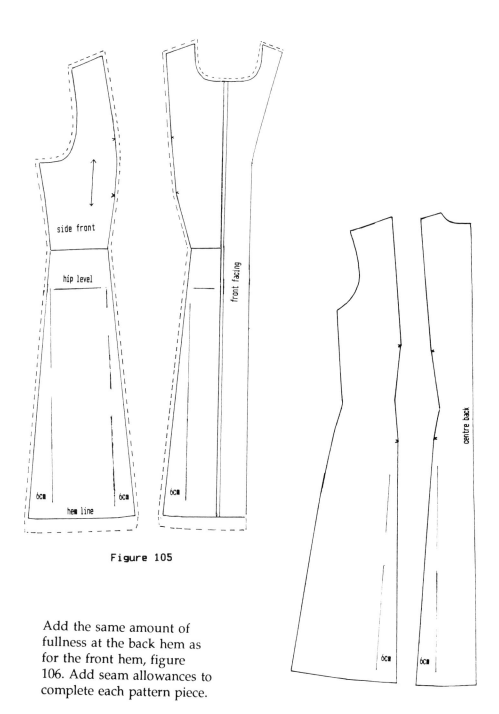

Figure 105

Add the same amount of
fullness at the back hem as
for the front hem, figure
106. Add seam allowances to
complete each pattern piece.

Figure 106

The Wing Seam

To make a pattern for the wing seam style take a copy of the block above the waist line with the enlarged front dart. Draw in the line for the wing seam as shown with a broken line, figure 107. Cut this out, cut out the dart, and cut along the wing style line to within 0.2cm of the apex of the dart. Close the dart slightly, opening up the new dart as shown in figure 108. Draw a grain line to run parallel to the centre front and mark notches at the apex of the dart. Shorten the new dart as shown and mark a notch at the apex. The apex of each dart should be about 12cm apart. Connect the darts with a broken line as shown in figure 108.

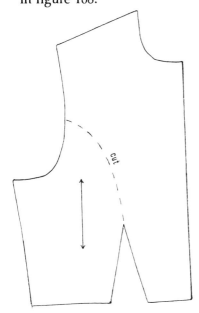

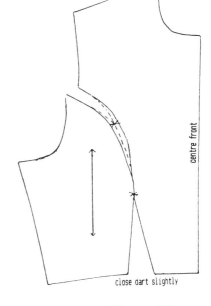

cut

centre front

close dart slightly

Figure 107

Figure 108

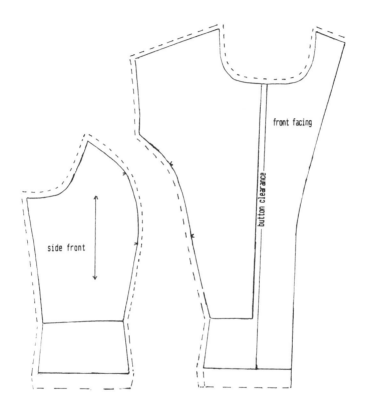

Figure 109

Cut out the darts and cut along the broken line separating the two pieces. Redraw each piece and extend the length to the desired style as described for the Princess line. Add seam allowances and front button clearance with built on facing, figure 109. To adapt this pattern to a full length dress follow the same procedure as described for the Princess line dress.

POCKETS

Welt and Piped Pocket

For both welt and piped pockets a pocket bag is required. The bags are usually cut in two sections, one in lining and one in self fabric. The size of the lining bag needs to be 2.5cm wider than the intended pocket opening by the desired depth of the pocket. The self fabric bag should be the same width as the lining but 1cm more in depth. Round off the corners along one edge of each piece, figure 110.

Welt Pocket

Figure 111

pocket bag

Figure 110

It is necessary to use an interlining in the welt especially when the fabric is cut on the bias as in figure 111. It is also advisable to reinforce the area of the garment at the pocket position by ironing a piece of interlining onto the wrong side of the garment, figure 112. To make the welt, cut a rectangle of fabric measuring 7cm by the length of the intended pocket opening plus 4cm. Iron the interlining to half the width as shown in figure 113. Fold lengthwise with right sides together and machine stitch the ends, figure 114.

Figure 112

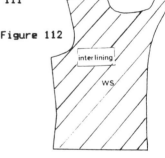

interlining

WS

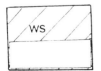

WS

Figure 113

welt

Figure 114

58

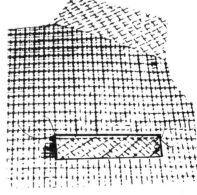

Figure 115

Turn and press the welt right side out. Mark the position for the pocket on the garment using tailors chalk. Place the raw edges of the welt to the marked pocket position on the garment. The right side of the welt should be placed to the right side of the garment. The interlined half being the top half. Machine the welt into position as in figure 115.

Place the pocket bags in position with the self fabric bag piece at the top with the straight edge against the marked pocket line. The lower, lining bag covering the welt with the raw edges together and the wrong side uppermost. Machine the bag onto the garment with two rows of stitching. The stitching rows should be 1.5cm apart as shown in figure 116. Turn the garment to the wrong side and cut an opening between the machine stitching. Snip diagonally into the corners as shown in figure 117. Take the pocket bag through the opening to the wrong side of the garment, figure 118. Pin and machine the pocket bag catching the clipped corners securely onto the pocket bag with forward and reverse stitching, figure 119. Neaten the pocket bag with overlocking or zig-zag stitch. Press the welt up and machine stitch into position on the right side of the garment. Secure with back stitching to strengthen the part of the pocket liable to the most strain.

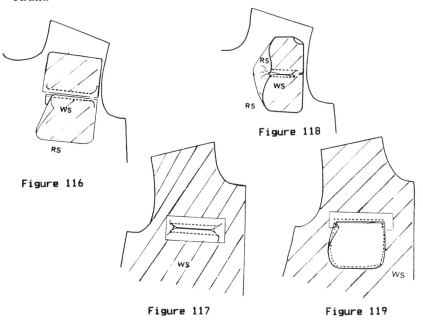

Figure 116

Figure 118

Figure 117

Figure 119

Piped Pocket

A piped pocket (figure 120) is
made in a similar way to the
welt pocket in that the piping
strips are stitched onto the
right side of the fabric first.
Mark the position of the pocket
with tailors chalk. Make the
piping strips by cutting a
strip of fabric measuring 2.5cm
by twice the length of the

Figure 120

pocket plus 5cm. Fold the strip in half lengthways with wrong
sides together and press. Cut the strips in half.

Next, pin the strips onto the garment with the raw edges together
along the marked pocket position and machine stitch exactly along
the centre of each strip starting and finishing 1cm from the
ends, figure 121.
Lay the pocket bags over the strips and stitch as described for
the welt pocket, figure 116. Follow the same procedure as
described for the welt pocket by cutting and turning the bag
through to the wrong side of the garment.
Reinforce the clipped corners, figure 122 and stitch the pocket
bag to finish. The folded edges will now come together on the
right side of the pocket to make a neat opening.

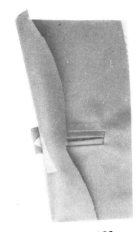

Figure 122

Figure 121

Side Panel Pocket

To make a pattern for this side
panel pocket draw round the
side front panel of either the
Princess line or wing seam
design. Draw the pocket onto
the pattern as shown with a
broken line in figure 124.

Now trace off the pocket piece, figure 125, and draw in a facing
line 3cm below the pocket line. Fold the paper along the top line
underneath the pocket and trace through the facing line. Open out
the paper and add seam allowances to the facing line, figure 126.

Now trace off the section of the pocket below the facing line and
add a seam allowance. This is the pocket bag lining pattern,
figure 127.

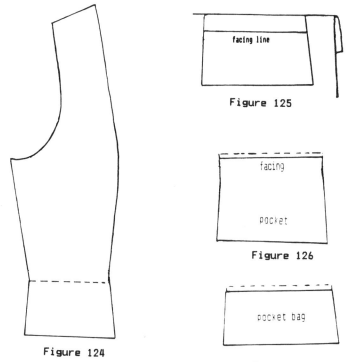

facing line

Figure 125

facing

pocket

Figure 126

pocket bag

Figure 127

Figure 124

To make up the pocket stitch the bag to the facing with right sides together. Now press the seam open and press the pocket along the fold line with wrong side of lining to wrong side of the pocket, figure 128.

Lay the pocket over the side panel and stitch the lining to this with right sides together along the hem line, figure 129. Trim away the excess lining at the hem line.

Now bring the pocket over the lining and stitch to the seam allowance of the side panel, figure 130. Continue to make up the garment in the usual way. Stitch the pocket into the side seam and the front seam. When turning the hem you may find it better to trim away some of the side panel at the hem and use the pocket piece as the hem. This way you will avoid too much bulk at the hem.

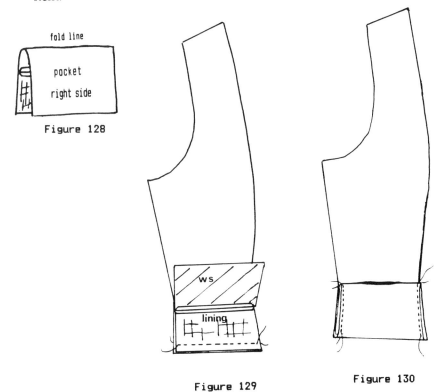

fold line

pocket

right side

Figure 128

w s

lining

Figure 129

Figure 130

Welt Panel Pocket

The welt panel pocket is cut in a similar way to the panel pocket. First take a copy of the side panel and draw on the pocket and welt as shown in figure 132.

Trace off the pocket and the welt separately and add seam allowances, figure 133. For each pocket you will need to cut two welt pieces and one pocket with a lining.

To make up, stitch one welt piece to the lining with right sides together and the other welt to the pocket with right sides together, figure 134. Press the seams open. Pin and stitch the welts together along the top, shaped, line with the right side of the pocket to the right side of the lining, figure 135.

Turn the pocket right side out and press the welt seam to the inside so that it does not show on the right side. Top stitch along the welt seam sinking the stitches into the channel where they will not be seen, figure 136. Stitch the pocket to the side front in the same way as described previously for the side panel pocket, figures 129 and 130.

Figure 133

Figure 132

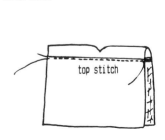

Figure 134

Figure 135

Figure 136

YOKES

Shirts and blouses are often
cut with a shoulder yoke.
The bodice may be cut with
any amount of fullness which
is gathered into the yoke.

First draw round the front blouse block and mark the desired
position of the yoke line. This line is really a matter of
personal choice but as a guide to its position a lowered shoulder
of between 6 and 10cm may be used. Mark crosses on this line to
use as balance notches. Also mark two vertical lines from the
yoke line to the hemline as shown in figure 139.
Cut this out and cut along the yoke line separating this from the
front bodice.
Place the front yoke shoulder line against the back shoulder line
as shown in figure 140.

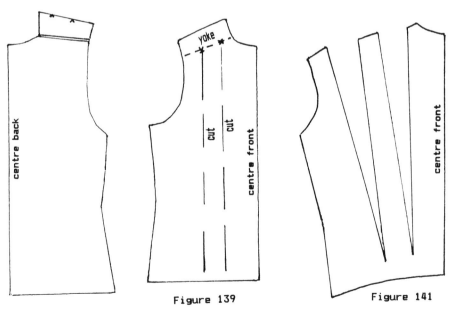

Figure 139

Figure 141

Figure 140

Now cut down the vertical lines on the front blouse from the yoke line to within 0.2cm of the hem line and open each cut as shown in figure 141. The amount of fullness is again a matter of personal choice but as a guide 4cm to 6cm may be used.
Redraw the outline and adjust the yoke line to a curved line and indicate that this is to be gathered into the yoke. Add the built on front facing and seam allowances to finish the pattern, figure 142.
Redraw the new back outline and add seam allowances as in figure 143. Record balance notches and shoulder line.
To make up gather the front blouse piece back to the original size and machine stitch this onto the yoke.

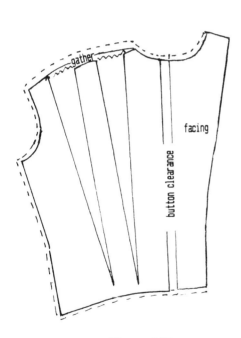

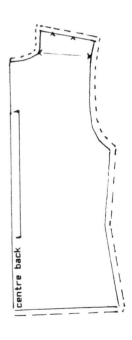

Figure 142   Figure 143

65

False Yoke

The blouse shown in figure 144 has a false yoke. This is an interesting feature and is cut in a similar way to the yoke but is actually an additional piece of fabric laid over the blouse front before making up.

To cut the pattern take a copy of the blouse block and add seam allowances and front facing. Draw the shape of the false yoke onto the pattern as shown in figure 145. Mark a grain line parallel to the centre front and another on the yoke indicating that the yoke will be cut on the bias.
Trace off the yoke and record the grain line. Add a hem allowance, figure 145a.

When making up this blouse hem the edge of the yoke first. Take extreme care not to stretch the fabric as it is bias cut and will have a tendancy to pull out of shape easily. If necessary a soft interfacing may be ironed onto the back of the yoke to prevent stretching. After hemming the yoke lay this over the shoulder area of the blouse with right sides of both yoke and blouse uppermost and machine stitch this in place within the seam allowances. Then continue to make up the blouse in the usual way.

Figure 144

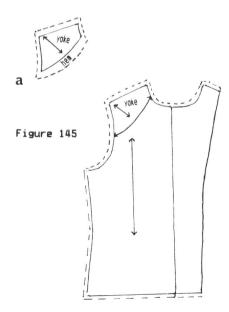

a

Figure 145

66

Neck and Front Yoke

To cut the pattern for a
contrast neck and front yoke
draw round the front blouse and
add the button clearance. Now
draw in the desired yoke line
as shown with a broken line in
figure 146.

Cut along the broken line
separating the contrast piece
from the main blouse. Redraw
the main blouse piece and add
seam allowances, figure 147.

Place the yoke pattern piece
with the front fold line along
a folded piece of paper and add
seam allowances, figure 148.

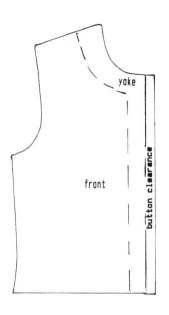

Figure 146

Figure 147

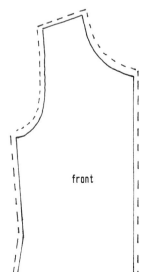

Cut this out and open the
pattern. The yoke now has a
built on facing, figure 149.
To make up first machine stitch
the yoke to the main blouse and
join the shoulder seams, figure
150. Bring the facing back over
the yoke with right sides
together and stitch around the
neckline as described for the
round neck in figure 24.

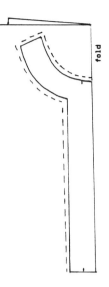

Figure 148

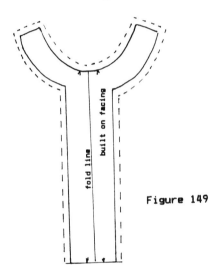

Figure 149

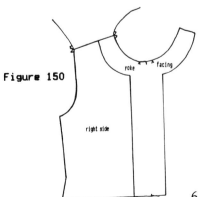

Figure 150

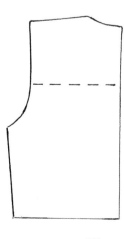

Figure 152

68

Back Yoke

For the back yoke with pleats below take a copy of the back blouse block and draw in the position of the desired yoke line as shown with a broken line in figure 152. Trace off the yoke and add seam allowances, figure 153.
Next fold the pleats into a piece of paper. Each pleat in figure 151 measures 2cm. You will therefore need to draw three vertical lines 2cm apart for each pleat and fold as shown in figure 154.
Cut along the yoke line and place the lower piece of pattern over the pleated paper. Draw round this and cut it out adding seam allowances. Open the pattern piece and mark the pleats, figure 155.

Figure 151

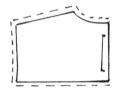

Figure 153

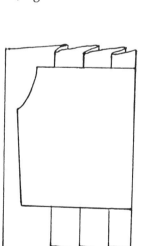

Figure 154

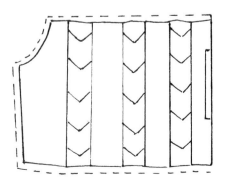

Figure 155

69

SIZING UP FOR THE JACKET.

The blouse block may be used for a jacket but because jackets are worn over other light clothing it is necessary to enlarge the block allowing for a little more ease than the original 10cm. The area around the shoulder, bust, neck line, armhole and sleeve will all need extra ease. The simplest way to size up the pattern is to take a copy of the back, front and sleeve blocks and adjust these as shown in figures 157 and 158.

As you will see 0.2cm is added to the centre front and centre back respectively. The shoulder width is increased by 0.3cm and the shoulder end is raised by 0.3cm to accommodate shoulder pads. The armhole is re-shaped and lowered by 1.2cm as shown by a broken line in figure 157. The width at the side is increased by 1.2cm. Although these increases may seem to be small amounts they do add up to another 5.6cm of ease on top of the original 10cm around the bust circumference on the whole pattern.

Figure 156

70

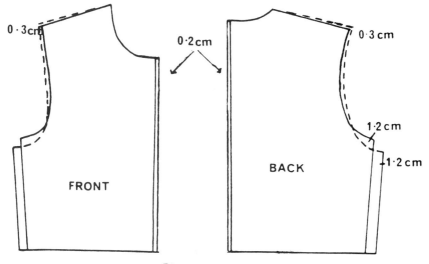

Figure 157

Figure 158

The sleeve has been cut along the centre line and 1.5cm has been added here. The underarm part of the sleeve head has been extended by 1cm and lowered by the same amount as shown with a broken line in figure 158. This line is now shaped into the original wrist line as shown which in effect increases the wrist circumference by only 1.5cm.

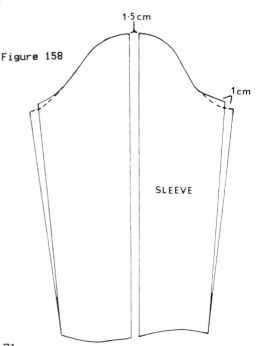

To make the pattern for the jacket shown in figure 156 you must
first convert the jacket block to the wing seam pattern as
described in figures 107 to 108. Decide upon the length for the
jacket and then draw on the front shaping. The length and shaping
is a matter of personal choice but the length of the jacket in
figure 156 is extended by 8cm below the waist at the side seam
and slants to 9cm longer at the wing seam. The lower front point
is 6cm longer than the wing seam. The jacket is double breasted
therefore a clearance of 8cm is allowed to the right of the
centre front. The buttons are positioned about 4cm above the
waist and this is the position of the front shaping. The front
shaping is illustrated with the longer broken lines in figure
159. Draw a facing line onto the pattern piece as shown.
Trace off the facing and add seam allowances, figure 160. Add
seam allowances to the side and front panels of the jacket,
figure 161.

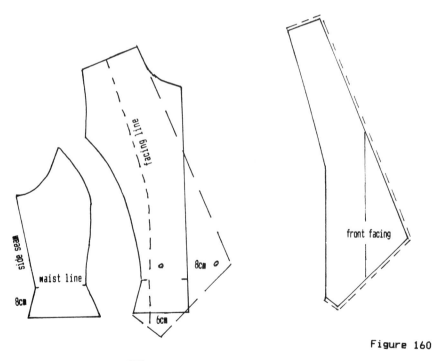

Figure 160

Figure 159

72

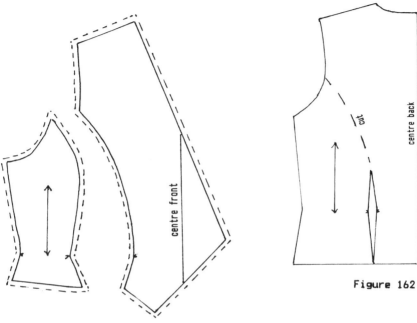

Figure 161

Figure 162

The back of the jacket is cut from the jacket block with a wing seam running through to match the front. For this draw round the back block and mark the dart. Draw a curved line from the apex of the dart towards to the armhole, figure 162. Cut this out and separate the two pieces. Redraw and add seam allowances to complete the pattern piece, figure 163. Cut a back neck facing as described in figure 16.

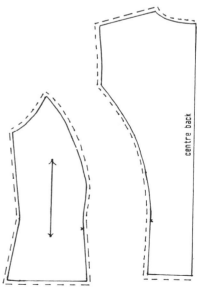

Figure 163

When making up the jacket machine the wing seams first, press
open and neaten. It is sometimes best to overlock each piece as
soon as it is cut then all the edges are neatened before being
joined. Another way is to stitch the seam and overlock at the
same time as described in figure 12. It is important that the
seams are finished neatly if the jacket is unlined. Iron a
suitable interfacing onto the wrong side of the facing. Stitch
the shoulder seams of the jacket and facing. Lay the facing over
the jacket with right sides together. Pin into position matching
the shoulder seams and machine stitch all round the front edge
and back neck, figure 164. Turn the facing to the inside of the
garment and press the seam towards the inside so that it is not
seen on the outside of the jacket. Set the sleeves in and stitch
thin shoulder pads around the sleeve crown. The hem is overlocked
to neaten the raw edge and then turned up and top stitched.

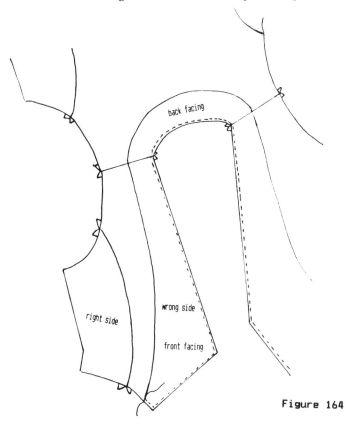

back facing

right side

wrong side

front facing

Figure 164

74

WAIST COAT.

The pattern for this gentleman's waist coat is easily made and the waist coat may of course be worn by either sex. The measurements required are - chest circumference, nape to waist and the finished back length. The table below is a useful guide.

	Chest	Nape to Waist	Back Length
Small	96cm	46cm	58cm
Medium	102cm	48cm	60cm
Large	109cm	49cm	61cm

To make the construction frame, first draw a rectangle measuring the waist coat back length by half the chest plus 2cm.
Mark the left hand side of the rectangle centre back and the right hand side centre front, figure 166.
Mark the top left hand corner A.
Measure down the centre back from A for the length of the nape to waist and mark this B.
Measure from A to the chest line (small 29cm) (medium 30cm) (large 31cm) and mark this C.
D is midway between A and C.
Draw horizontal lines from B,C and D to meet the centre front line.
Divide the rectangle vertically into four equal sections as shown by the broken lines. For the purpose of identification these are labelled "back shoulder", "front shoulder" and "side seam".

On the top line of the rectangle measure 4.5cm each side of the back shoulder line and mark these points with dots. Draw a short horizontal line 1cm below the top line extending this line just beyond the position of the dots. Repeat this at the front shoulder position. Raise the dots nearest to the centre back and centre front above the line by 2cm, figure 166.

This completes the construction frame and the waist coat pattern can now be formed upon this frame.

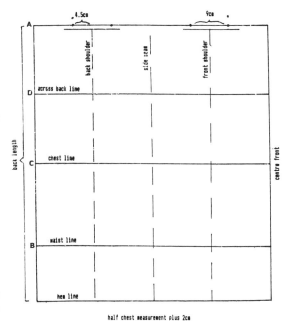

Figure 166

For the shoulder line, position the end of the metre stick at the raised dot and measure the waist coat shoulder width (small 8.5cm) (medium 9cm) (large 9.5cm) to meet the lower line. Draw in the shoulder line.

For the back and front armhole, drop vertical lines from the end of the shoulders to meet the across back line. (These lines should be a right angles to the top line).

For the back armhole continue the straight line beyond the cross back line for 2cm before you begin to shape the armhole with a curve. As a guide the curve should be approximately 5cm out from the right angle, figure 167.

For the front armhole continue the line below the across back line by 7cm before drawing the curved line. A suggested guide of 3cm from the right angle is given here. The front armhole should be flatter at the underarm position and it is advisable to draw along the chest line for 3cm or 4cm before curving into the shaping

76

Draw in the back neck from the shoulder to the centre back. The centre back of the neck should be flat for 3cm before curving towards the shoulder.
Draw a line from the shoulder to meet the chest line for the V neck.

The shaping of the waist coat is mainly created by the back belt and buckle but a little shaping may be incorporated in the pattern at the side seam position. To achieve this shaping measure 1.5cm each side of the side seam line at the waist line and draw in new side seams to meet the armhole and hem line respectively.

The pocket position should be 1cm above the waist line. The size of the welt is 10cm x 2.5cm and this should be drawn with 5cm each side of the front shoulder line.

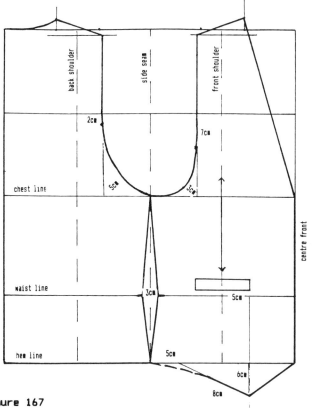

Figure 167

To find the position of the front points, draw a vertical line from the edge of the pocket and extend this line 6cm below the hem line. Connect the point to the centre front with a straight line. The hemline coming from the side seam should have a gentle curve. To achieve this curve first draw a straight line from the point to a position on the hem 5cm from the side seam. Draw in the point measuring 8cm and then curve the line to the side seam as shown by a broken line.

Mark a grain line along the vertical front shoulder line. Trace off each piece separately and add seam allowances. Add a button clearance of 2cm to the centre front. Indicate that the centre back should be placed to the fold, figure 168.
The back of a waist coat is usually cut in lining. The waist coat in figure 165 does not have a facing but a front lining serves as the facing. The waist coat is fully lined. Therefore the back will require cutting twice in lining and the fronts will also require a lining.

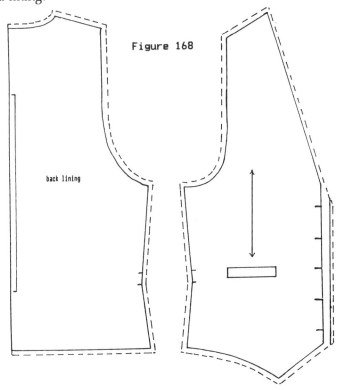

Figure 168

back lining

INDEX

Armhole 8, 12, 19, 43, 48, 51, 70, 73, 76
Balance notches 5, 17, 33, 44, 47, 50, 64, 65
Belt 77
Bias 38, 58, 66
Binding 38
Bust 6-8, 10, 70
Button clearance 16, 24, 35, 39, 57, 67
Buttonholes 3, 22, 23
Chalk 5, 20, 22, 59, 60
Check 6, 9, 11, 13, 14, 20, 54
Chest 6, 9, 14, 75-77
Collar 3, 30-38, 41
Cuff 3, 42, 43, 49
Darts 3, 4, 10, 17, 18, 52-54, 56, 57
Design 2, 4, 24, 61
Dress 3, 4, 30, 47, 54, 57
Ease 4, 6-10, 12, 14, 19, 20, 22, 23, 43, 52, 70
Elbow 6, 12-14, 20
Equipment 5
Facing 16, 21, 24-29, 32-36, 40, 65, 66, 72-74, 78
Fitting 19, 30, 52
Flaws 17
Gather 43, 65
Hem 15, 16, 23, 33, 45, 49, 54, 55, 62, 65, 74, 78
Hip 6, 10, 11
Interfacing 29, 32, 34, 66, 74
Iron 5, 17, 29, 32, 34, 41, 58, 74
Jacket 3, 4, 47, 54, 70, 72-74
Lining 5, 58, 59, 61-63, 78
Marking 3, 17
Neckline 3, 24-29, 32, 36, 38, 68
Notches 5, 17, 31-35, 44, 47, 50, 53, 56, 64, 65
Overlock 5, 15, 17, 19, 23, 32, 33, 36, 38, 74
Panel 3, 47, 61-63
Pleat 50, 51, 69
Pocket 3, 58-63, 77, 78
Princess line 3, 52-54, 57, 61
Seam allowance 15, 19, 20, 32, 61
Selvedge 17

Sleeve 3, 6, 12-15, 18-20, 23, 36, 42-44, 46-51, 70, 74
Tailors chalk 5, 22, 59, 60
Test Cloth 4
Thread 5, 19, 38, 45
Tracing 3, 5, 14, 16, 17, 35
Underwear 6, 25
V neck 26
Waist coat 3, 75-78
Waist line 7, 8, 10, 54, 56, 77
Welt 3, 58-60, 63, 77
Wing seam 3, 52, 56, 61, 72, 73
Wrist 6, 13, 20, 42, 43, 50, 71
Yoke 3, 64-69
Zig-zag 5, 17, 32, 38, 59

Other Titles by Brenda Redmile

40 Skirts to Cut and Sew

The Tops

Brenda Redmile runs short courses in Dress Design and Pattern Making at various residential colleges throughout Britain. If you are interested in attending any of her courses write for details to Spawton Books enclosing a stamped and self addressed envelope.

For details of other books on dressmaking write to Spawton Books enclosing a stamped and self addressed envelope.